BASTIEN PIANO BASICS
SUPPLEMENTARY

Popular Christmas Songs
LEVEL 2

ARRANGED BY JAMES BASTIEN

kjos NEIL A. KJOS MUSIC COMPANY • SAN DIEGO, CALIFORNIA

Dear teachers and parents:

The Christmas holiday season is an exciting time of the year, and students will enjoy playing the wide variety of carols provided in **Popular Christmas Songs**.

The carols are arranged in a progressive order of difficulty from easy to more difficult. Full-color illustrations entertain along the way.

We offer you our best wishes for a Merry Christmas!

Neil A. Kjos Music Company
James Bastien
Jane Smisor Bastien

ISBN 0-8497-9309-2

© 1986 Kjos West, 4382 Jutland Drive, San Diego, California 92117. International copyright secured. All rights reserved. Printed in U.S.A.
WARNING! All the music, text, art and graphics in this book are protected by copyright law. To copy or reproduce them by any method is an infringement of the copyright law. Anyone who reproduces copyrighted matter is subject to substantial penalties and assessments for each infringement.

Contents

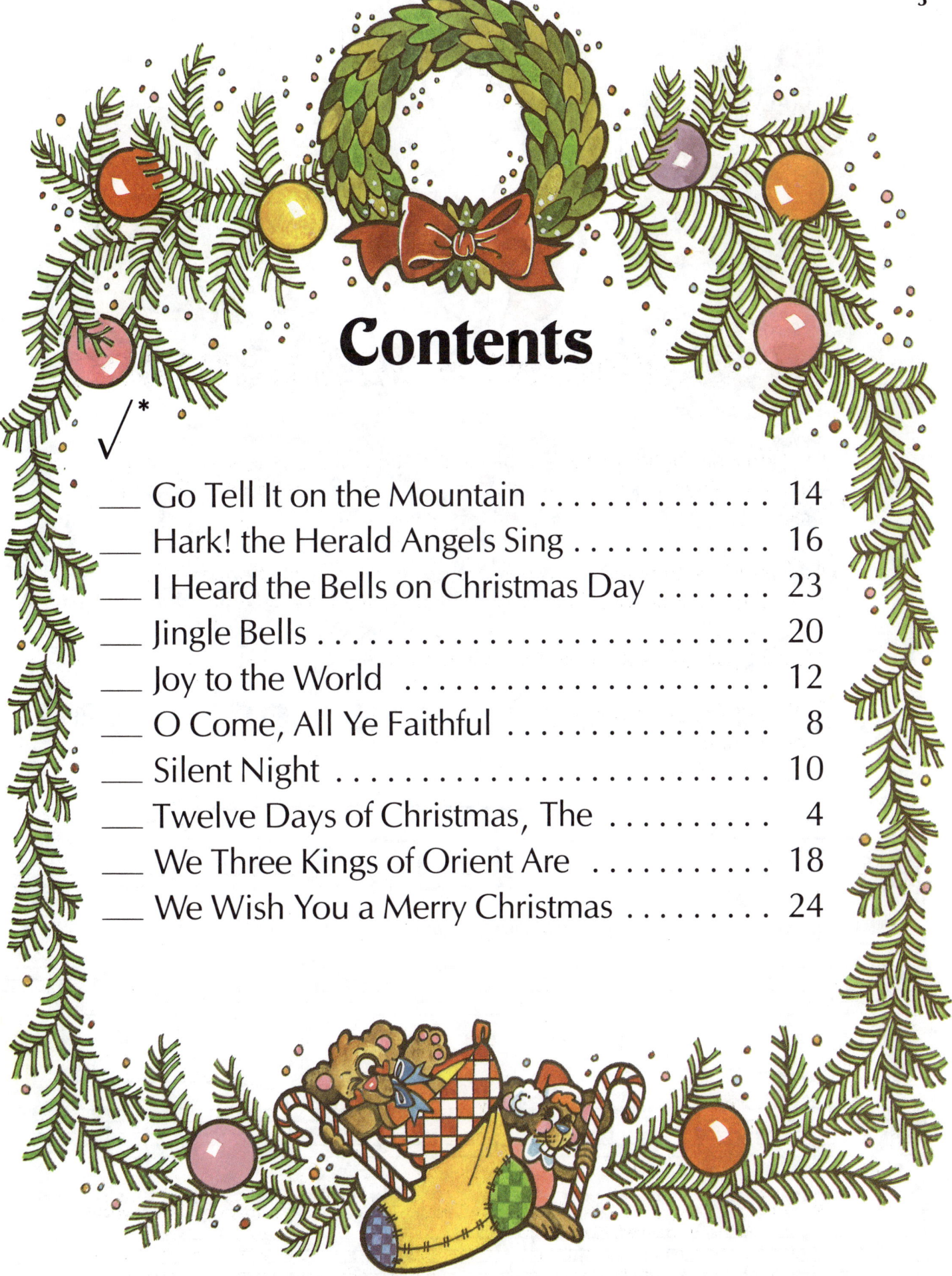

√*

___ Go Tell It on the Mountain 14
___ Hark! the Herald Angels Sing 16
___ I Heard the Bells on Christmas Day 23
___ Jingle Bells 20
___ Joy to the World 12
___ O Come, All Ye Faithful 8
___ Silent Night 10
___ Twelve Days of Christmas, The 4
___ We Three Kings of Orient Are 18
___ We Wish You a Merry Christmas 24

*To reinforce the feeling of achievement, the teacher or student may put a √ when the page has been mastered.

WP222

The Twelve Days of Christmas

Moderato Traditional

WP222

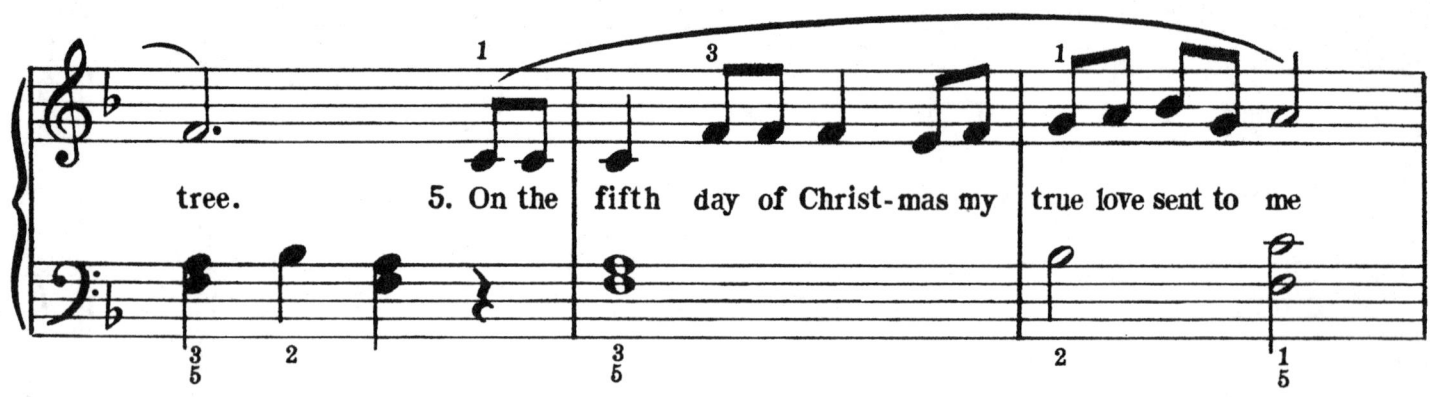

Repeat this measure and sing in reverse order beginning with "seven swans a swimming."

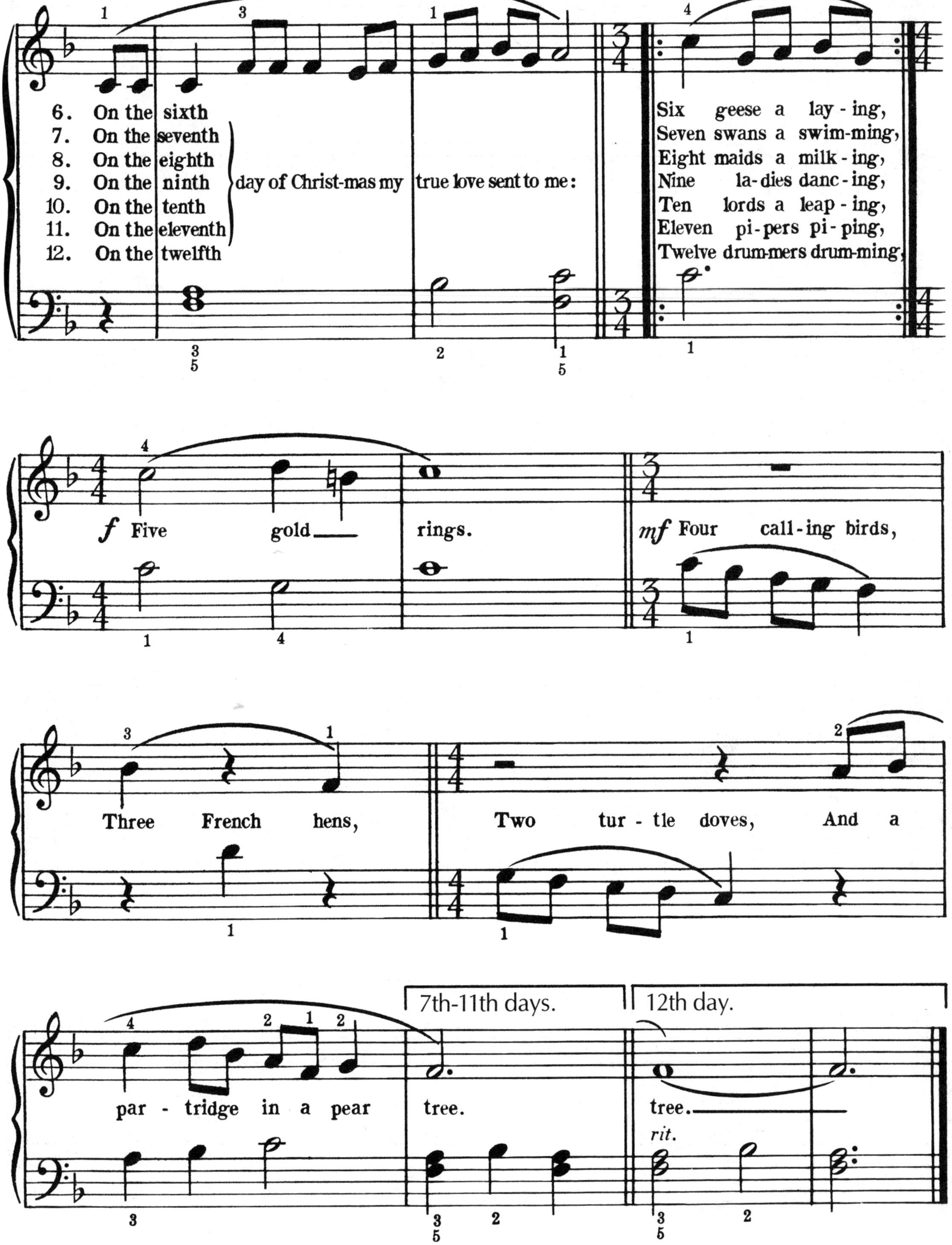

Repeat from the top of the page for the 7th through 11th days.

O Come, All Ye Faithful
(Adeste Fideles)

Moderato

J.W. Wade

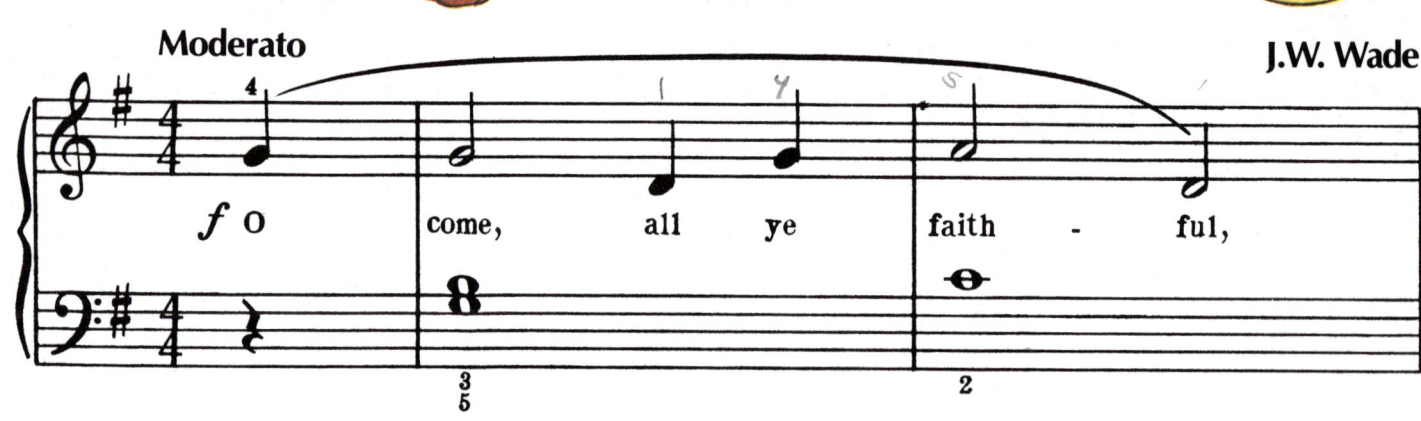

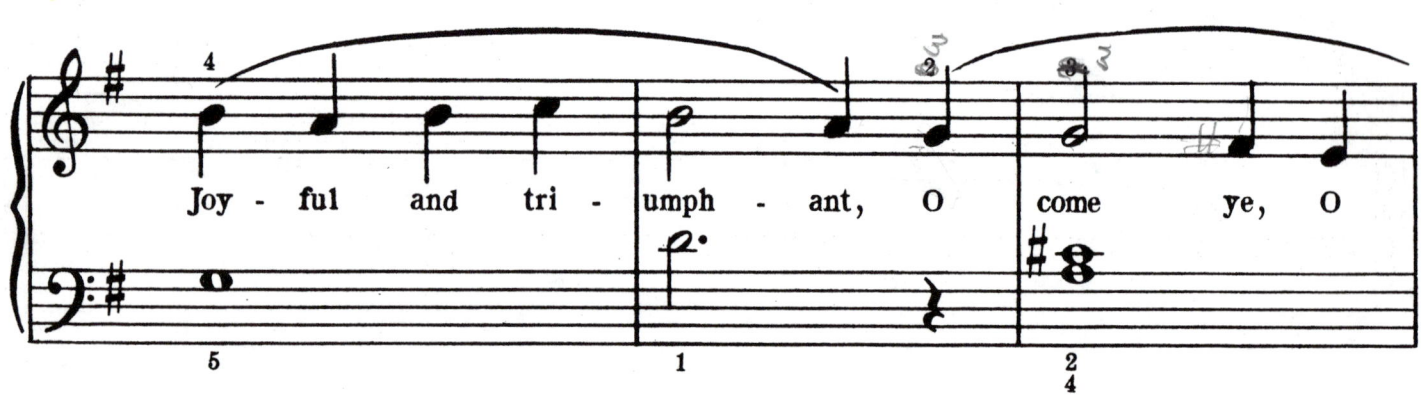

WP222

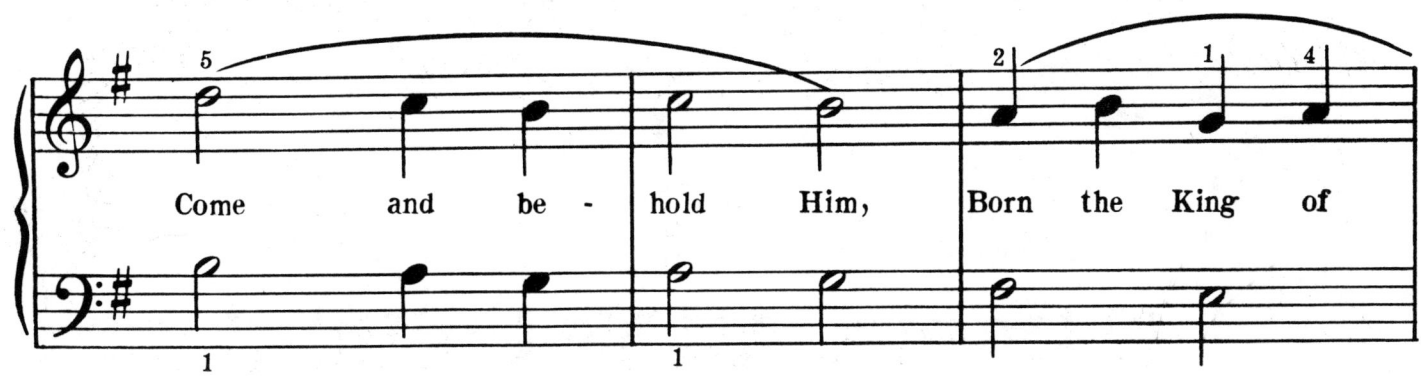

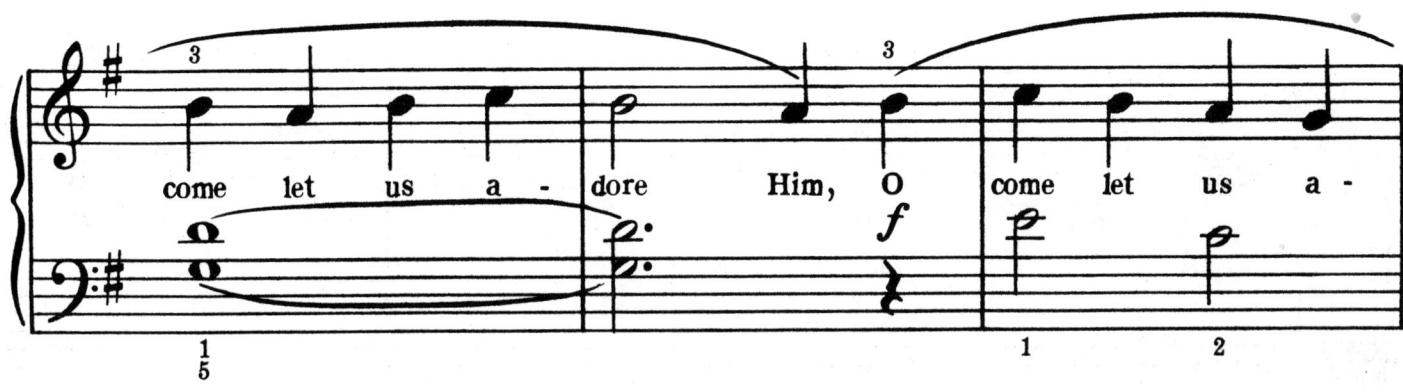

Silent Night

Andante — Franz Gruber

p Si - lent night! Ho - ly night!

All is calm, All is bright,

WP222

Joy to the World

With spirit   George F. Handel

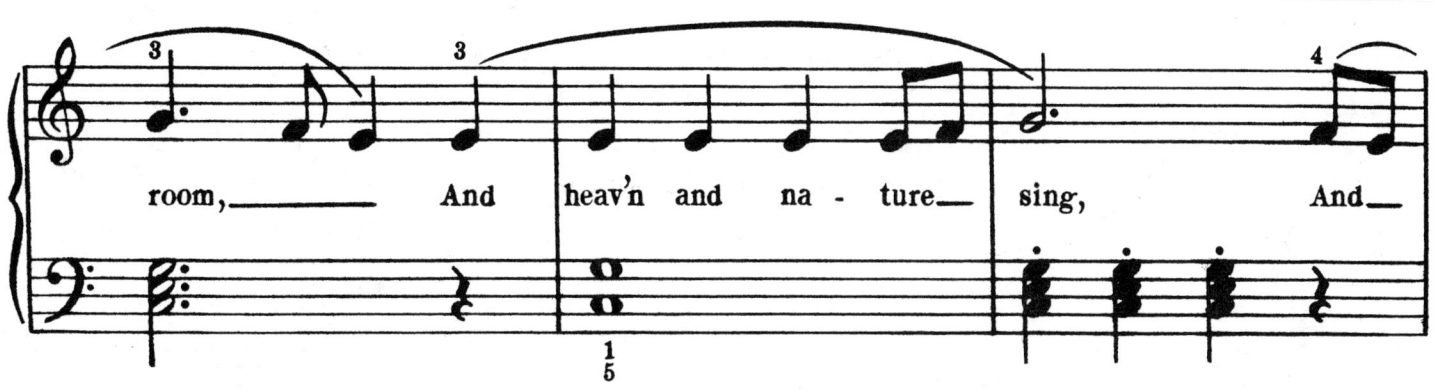
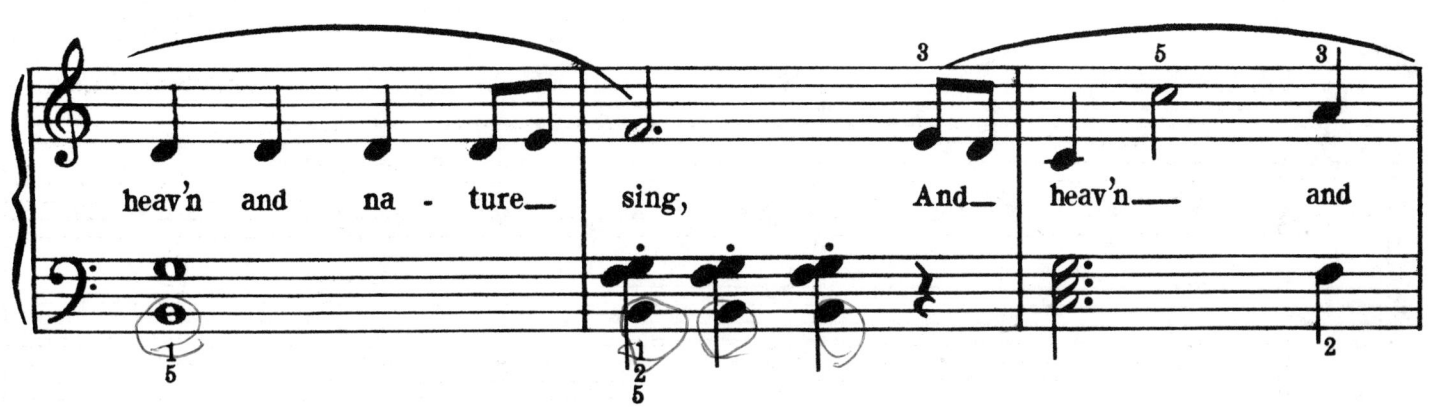
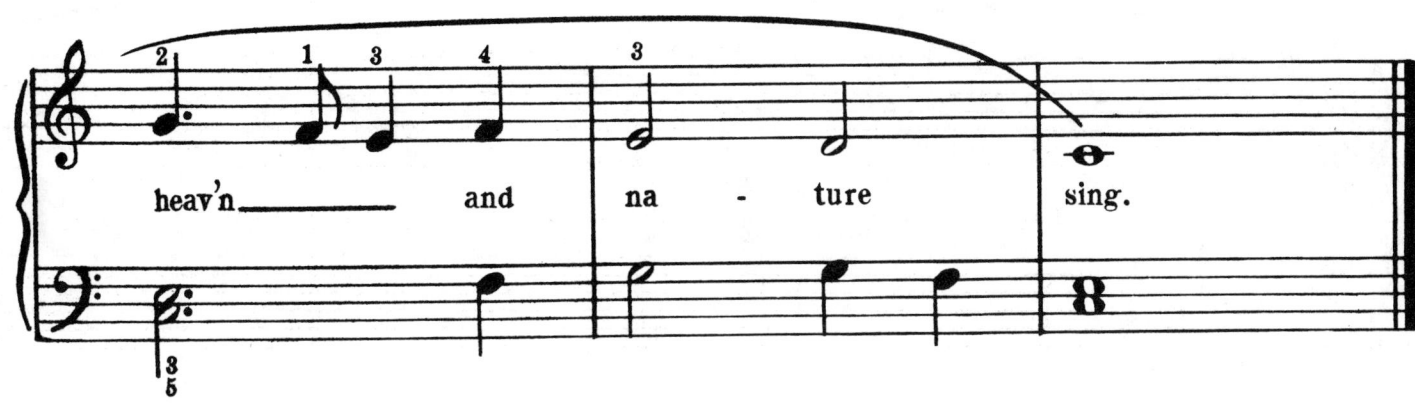

WP222

Go Tell It on the Mountain

With spirit   **Traditional**

mf Go tell it on the moun-tain, o-ver the hills and

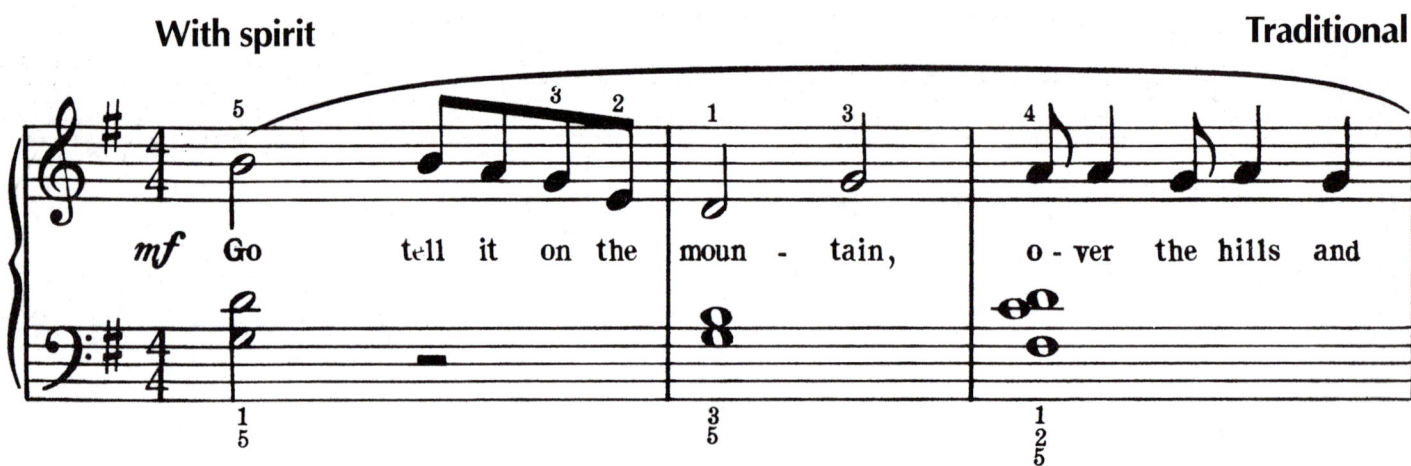

ev-'ry where; Go tell it on the moun-tain, that

Je-sus Christ is born! (A-men.) When I was a

WP222

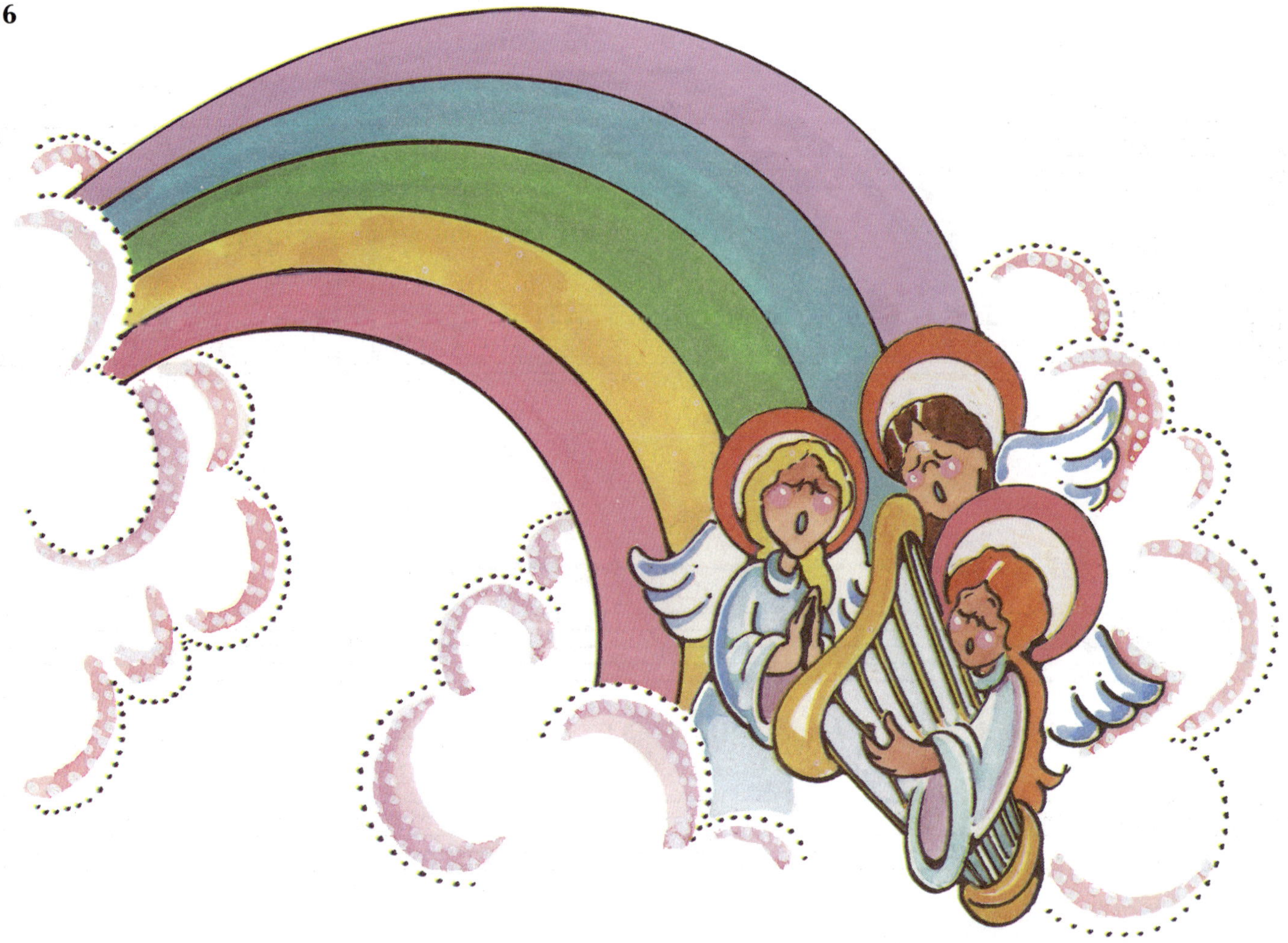

Hark! the Herald Angels Sing

With spirit

Felix Mendelssohn

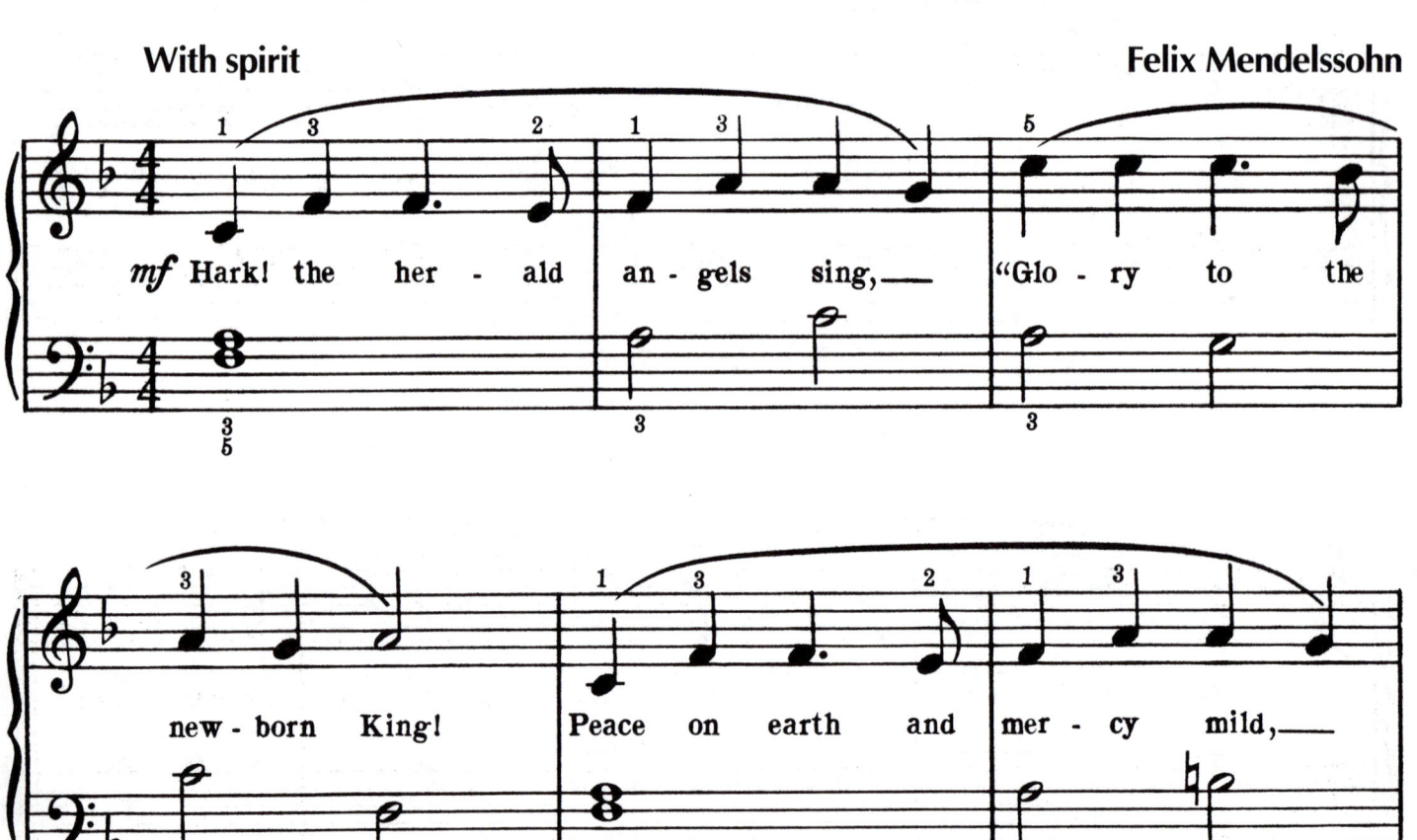

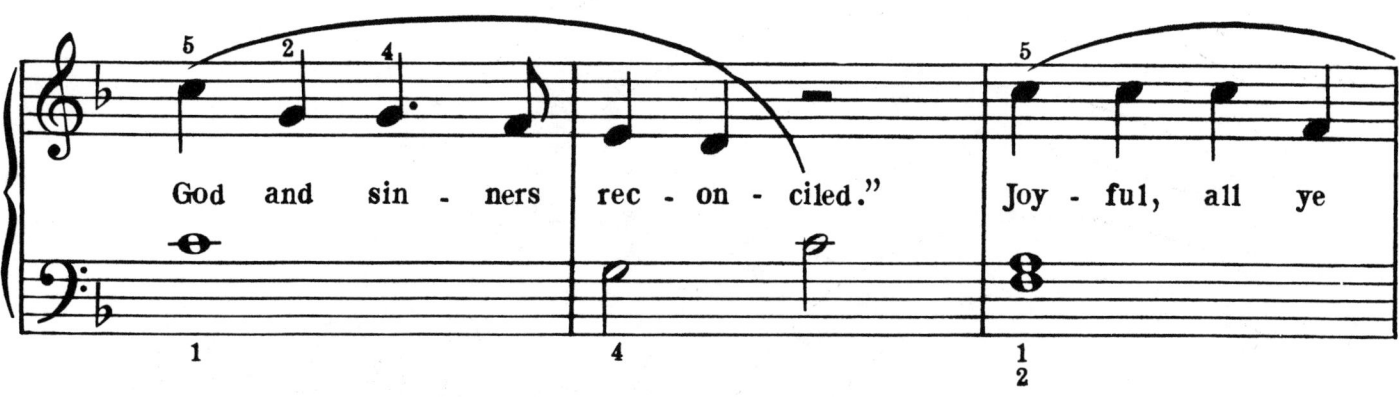

We Three Kings of Orient Are

Moderato

John H. Hopkins

We three Kings of O-ri-ent are;

Bear-ing gifts we trav-erse a-far.

Field and foun-tain, moor and moun-tain,

WP222

Fol - low - ing yon - der star.
O Star of
won - der, star of night,
Star with roy - al
beau - ty bright,
West - ward lead - ing, still pro -
ceed - ing, Guide us to Thy per - fect light.

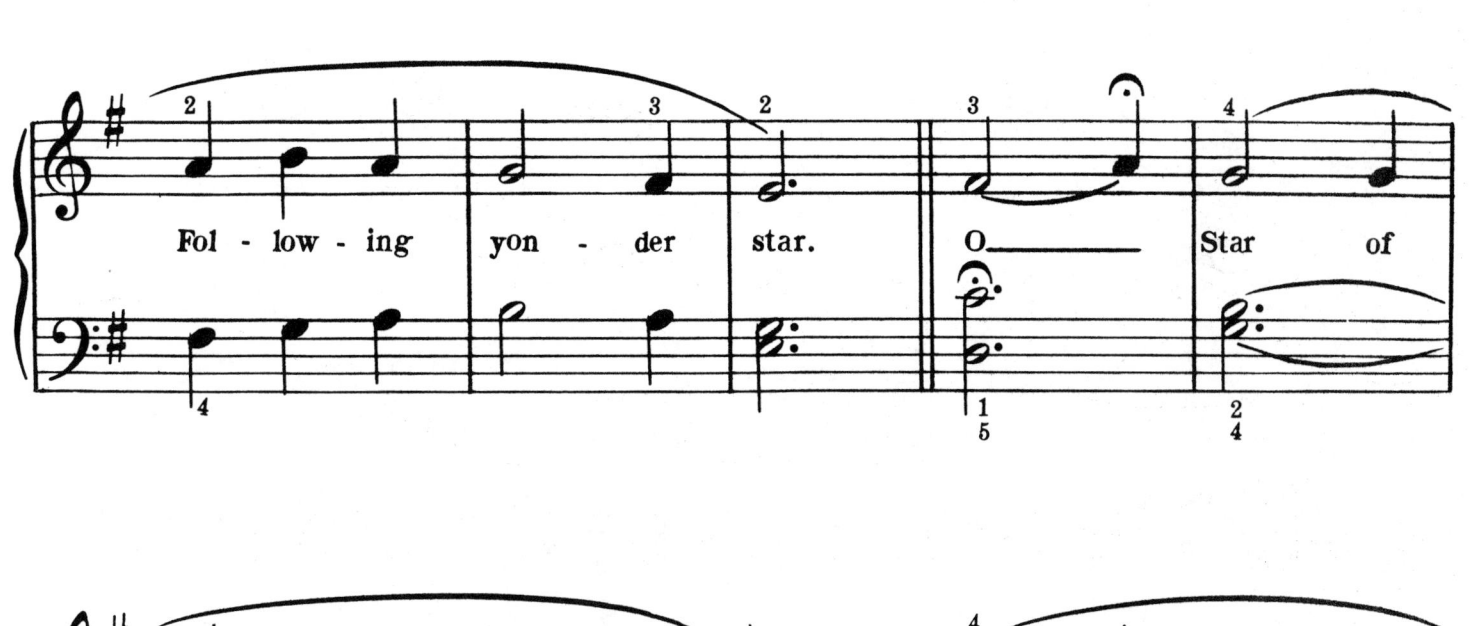

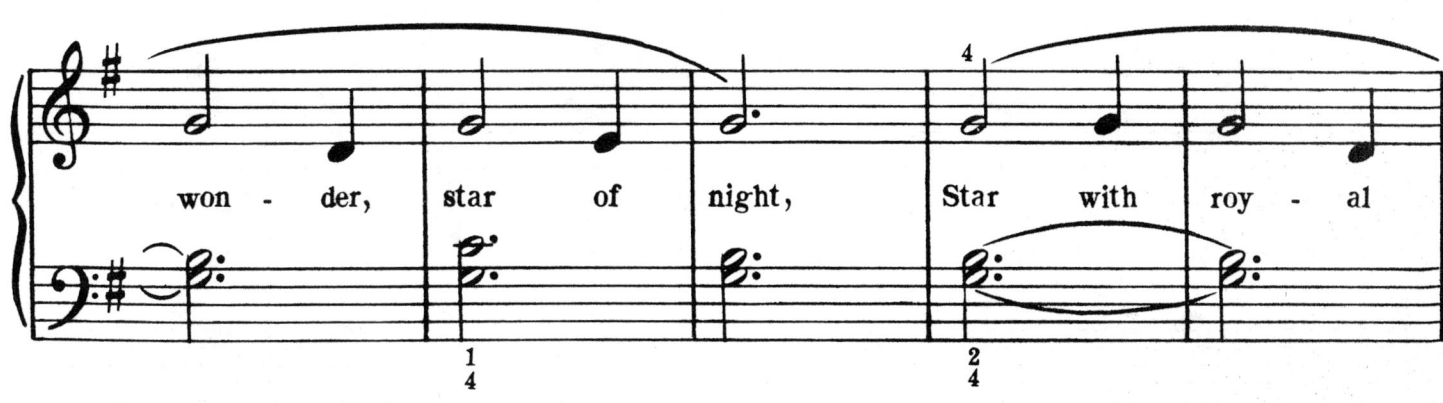

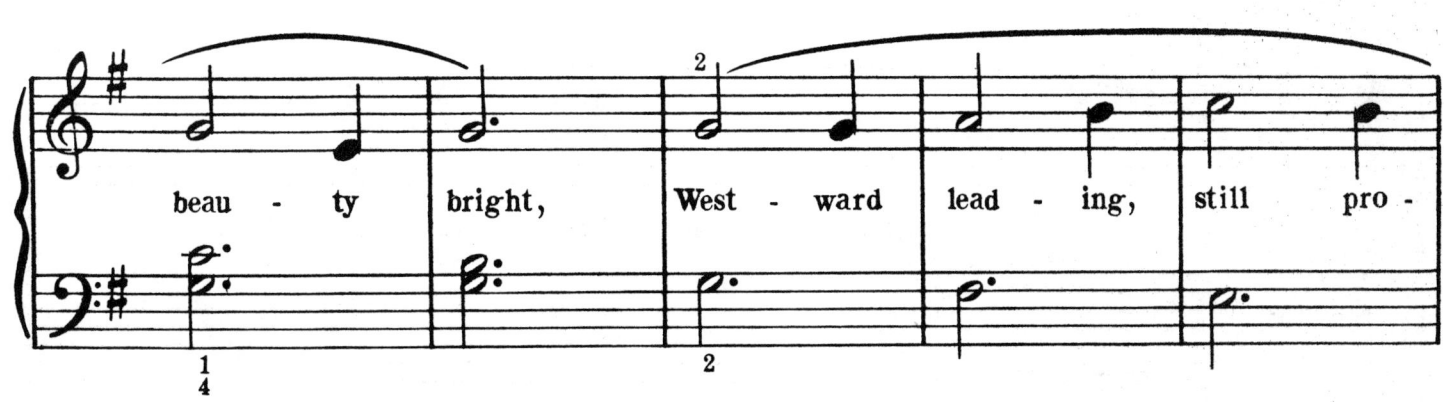

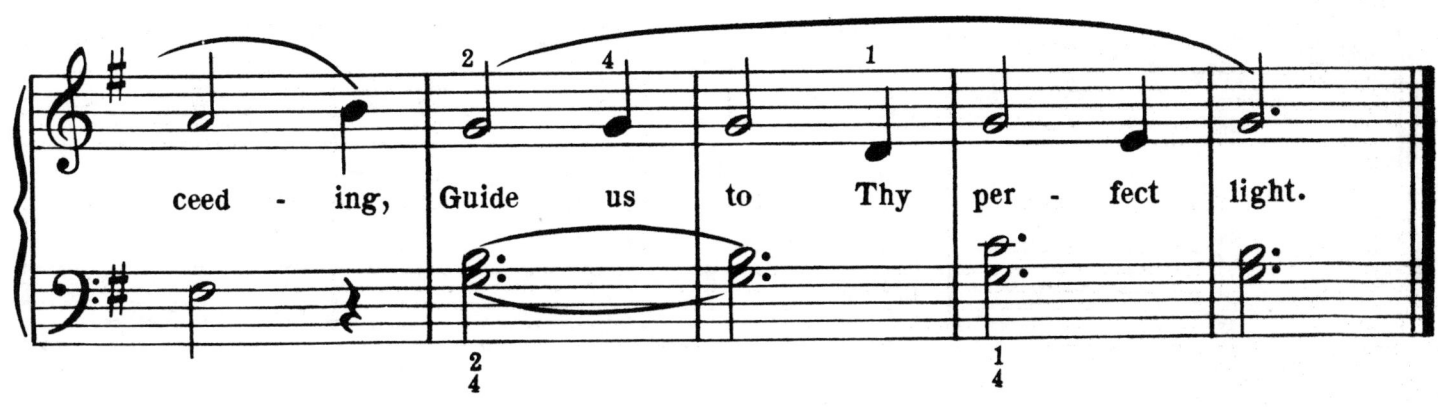

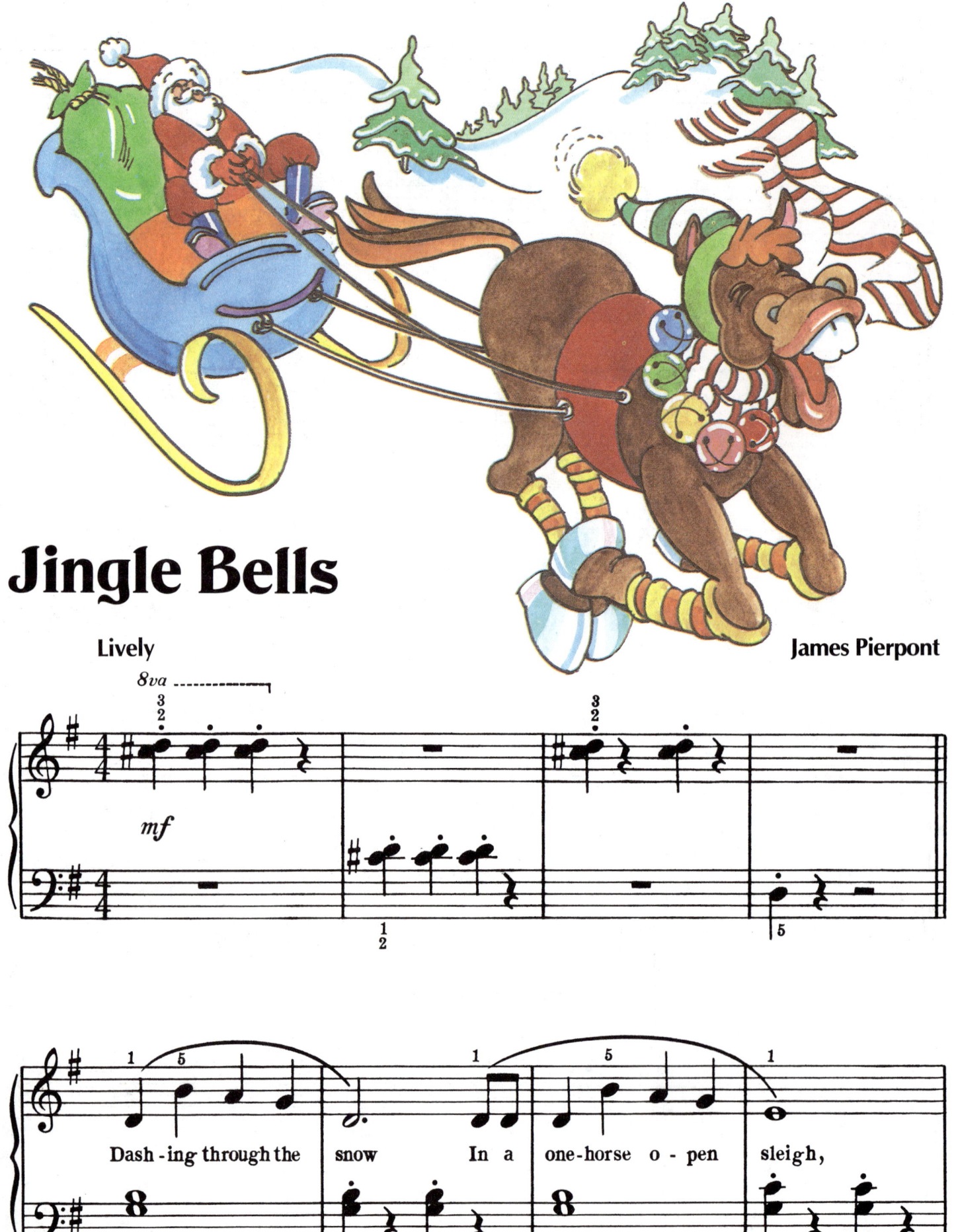

O'er the fields we go, Laugh-ing all the way.
Bells on bob-tail ring, Mak-ing spir-its bright, What
fun it is to ride and sing a sleigh-ing song to night!
f Jin-gle bells, Jin-gle bells, Jin-gle all the way!

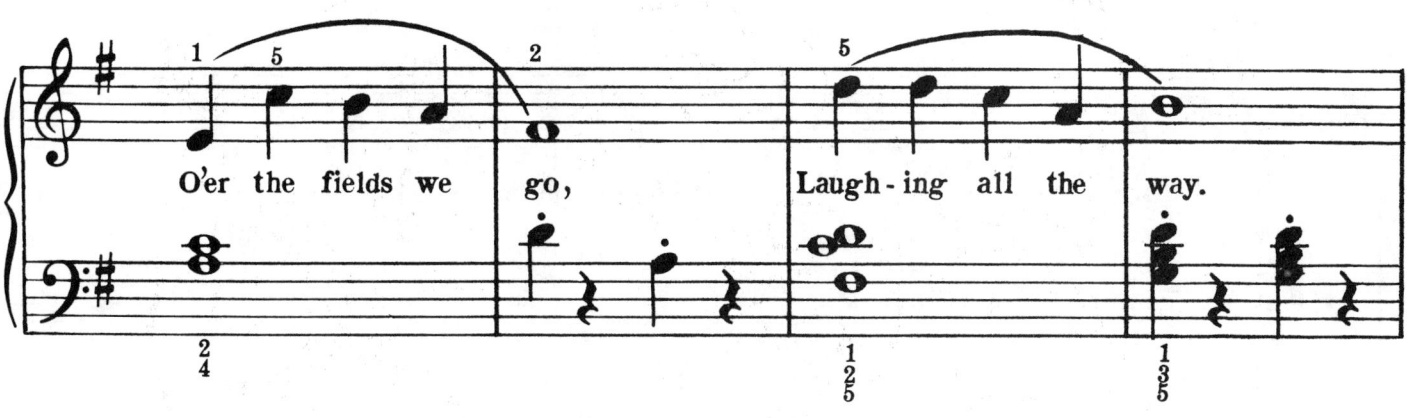

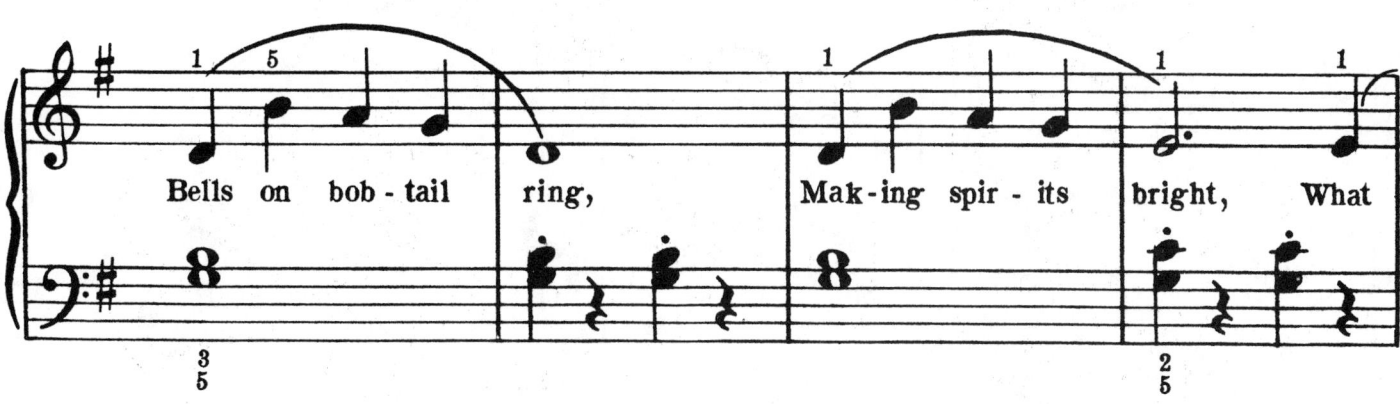

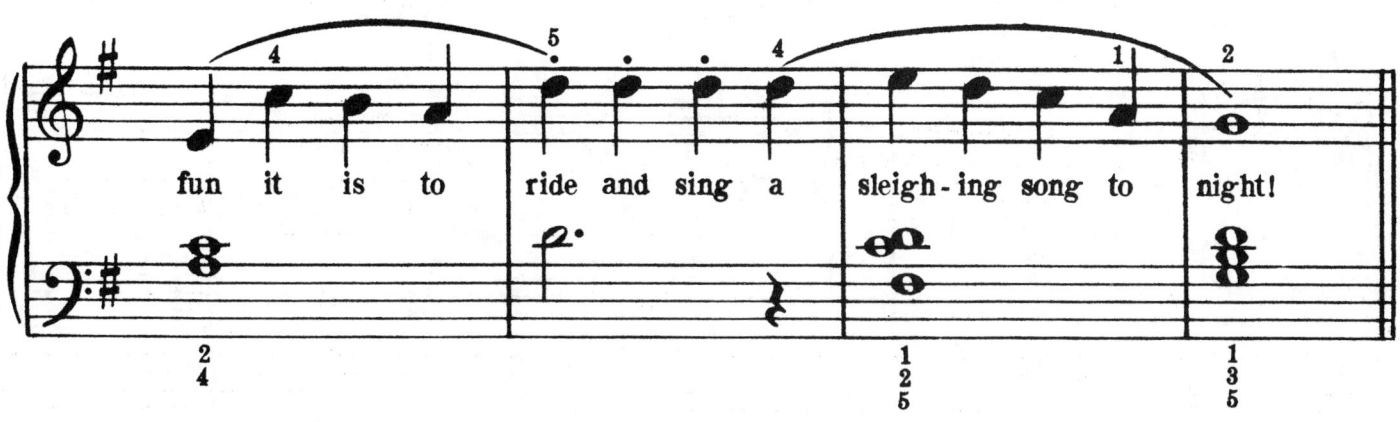

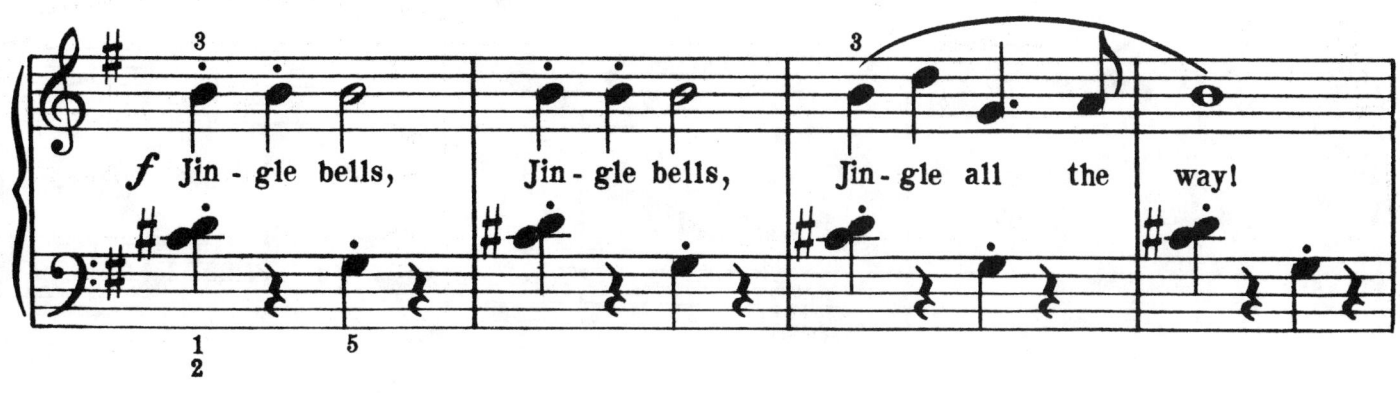

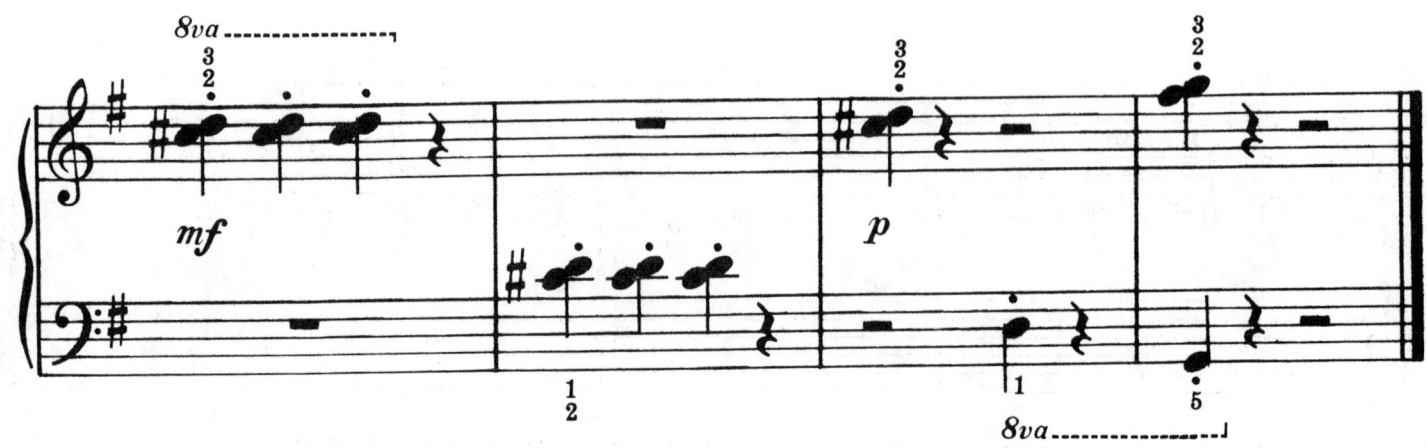

I Heard the Bells on Christmas Day

Moderato

J.B. Colkin

WP222

We Wish You a Merry Christmas

Lively
Traditional

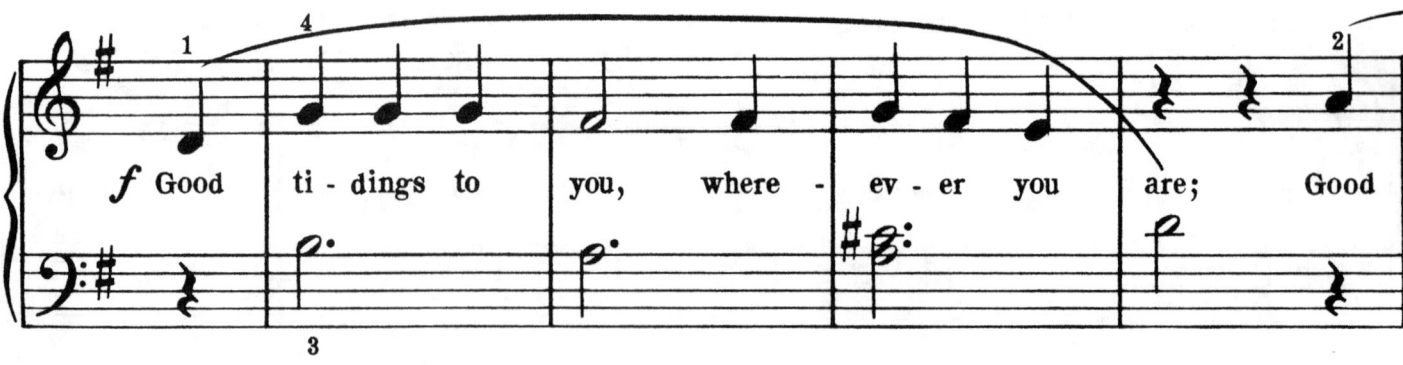

WP222